# Ink Doilies

### Angie's Patterns - Volume 1

©2012 Angie Grace. All rights reserved.

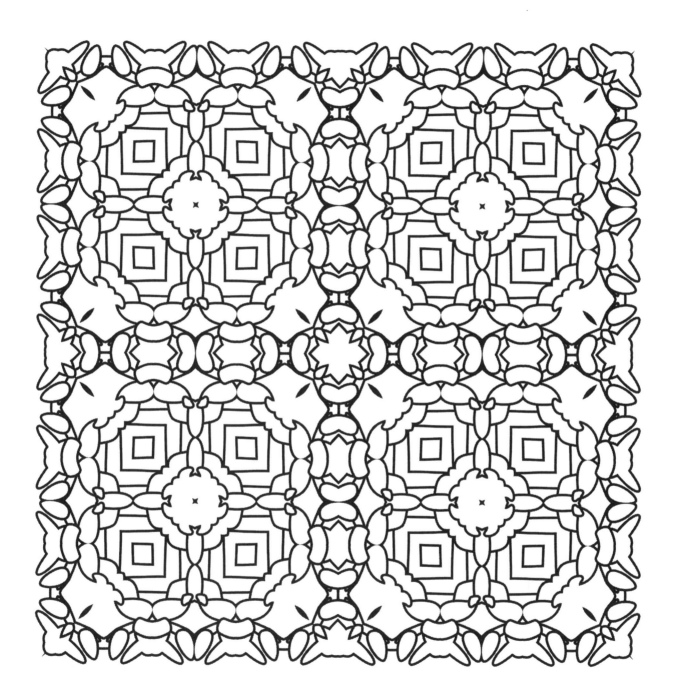

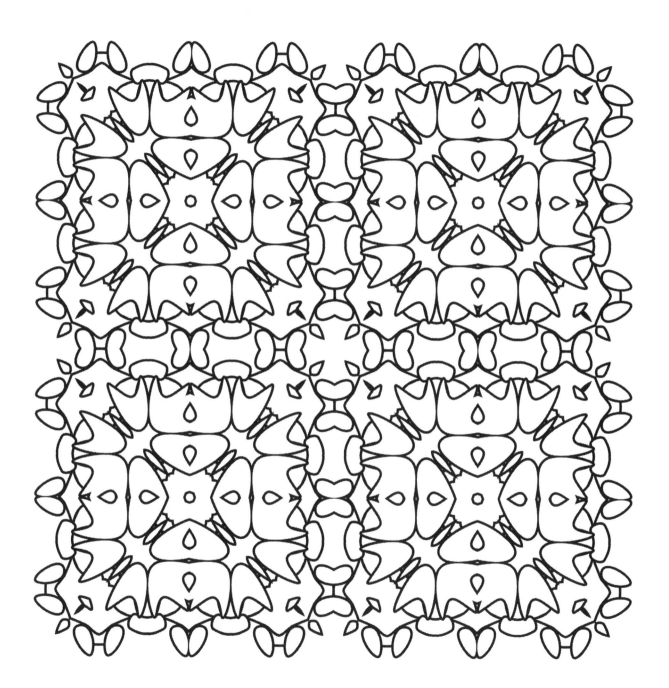

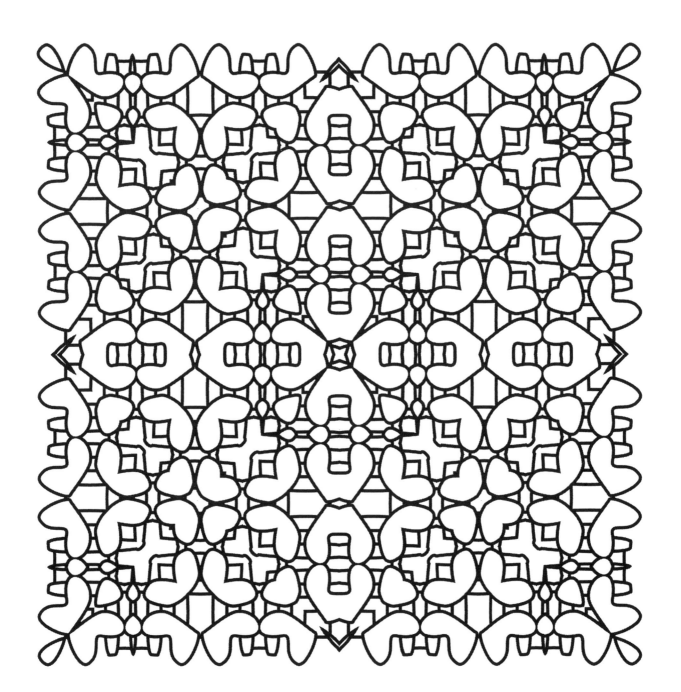

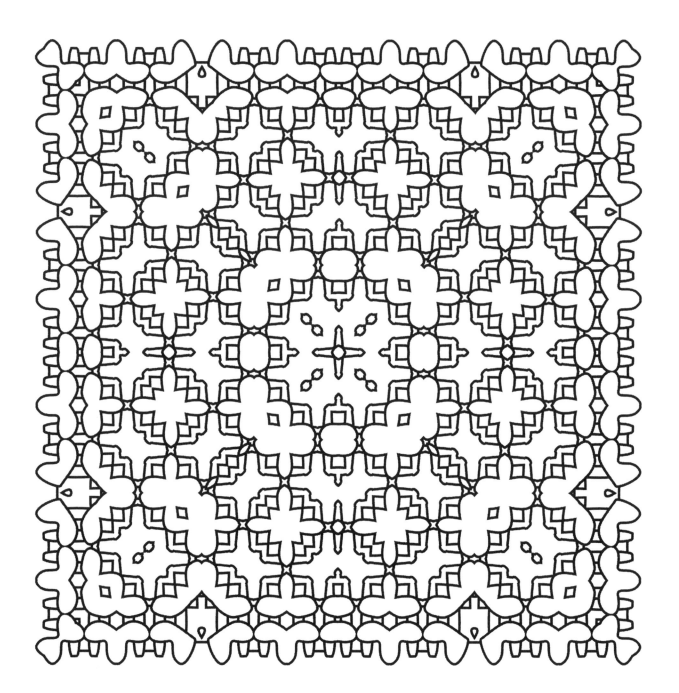

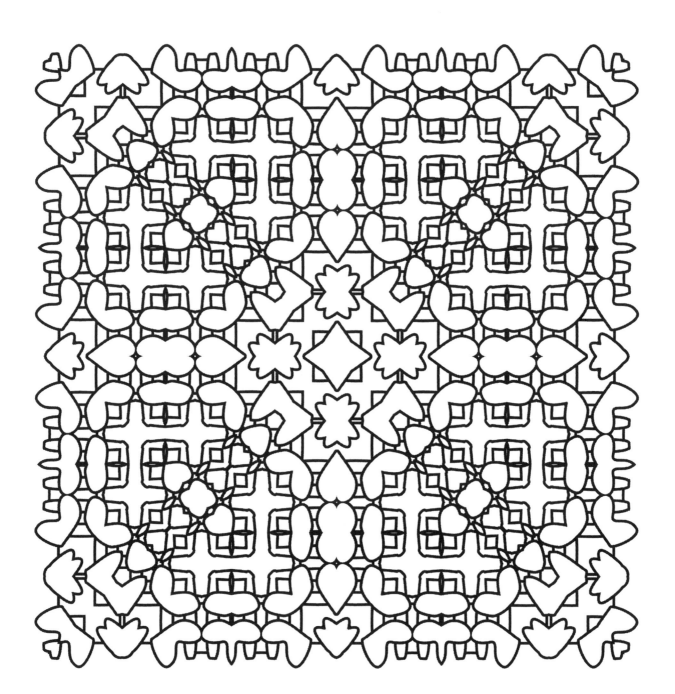

# Color With Angie & Friends

Join our friendly Color With Angie Grace Facebook group!

# www.AngieGrace.com

Visit Angie's website for special web exclusives for colorists.

Made in the USA
San Bernardino, CA
27 April 2015